Going Around The Corner
*A Guidebook To Be The ONE
Where You Live, Work & Play*

Todd & Sheila Alewine

Around The Corner Ministries exists to take the gospel to every neighborhood in America. Our mission is to equip followers of Jesus to engage their neighborhoods and communities with the gospel of Jesus Christ.

© 2019 by Todd & Sheila Alewine

All rights reserved. No part of this publication may be reproduced in any form without the written permission of Around The Corner Ministries, www.aroundthecornerministries.org

ISBN: 978-1-7330478-2-1

Scripture quotations taken from the New American Standard Bible® (NASB), Copyright © 1960, 1962, 1963, 1968, 1971, 1972, 1973, 1975, 1977, 1995 by The Lockman Foundation. Used by permission. www.Lockman.org.

Introduction

I am under obligation both to Greeks and to barbarians, both to the wise and to the foolish. So, for my part, I am eager to preach the gospel to you also who are in Rome. For I am not ashamed of the gospel, for it is the power of God for salvation to everyone who believes, to the Jew first and also to the Greek.
Romans 1:14-16

What would happen if you believed that a sovereign God has placed you where you are to be on mission for the spread of the gospel? That you are the ONE He strategically positioned at a specific time and place for particular people in whose hearts He is already working to draw them to Himself?

This book urges every follower of Christ to recognize our great obligation to those around us. Eternity is at stake, and our neighbors, co-workers, friends, classmates, and teammates need to hear the gospel. You have already been sent into the field. You are **O**bligated to your **N**eighbor's **E**ternity. God is calling you to be the ONE in your community—where you live, work, and play.

Hundreds of books have been written on how to share the gospel. There are plenty of scripts to memorize and strategies to execute, but unless we put them into practice, they will never reach a soul.

This little book is simply a tool, a guidebook, to help you take what you know about the gospel and share it. Take one step at a time and put it into action. Before you know it, you will love the people God has placed in your life with Christ's love and intercede in prayer for them. You will know them personally and be involved in their lives. You will feel confident in your own story of salvation and be able to share the complete gospel.

You will be the ONE to introduce them to Jesus.

STEP ONE
Believe God Has Put You Where You Are

> **KEY SCRIPTURE: Acts 17:24-26**
>
> *The God who made the world and all things in it, since He is Lord of heaven and earth, does not dwell in temples made with hands; nor is He served by human hands, as though He needed anything, since He Himself gives to all people life and breath and all things; and He made from one man every nation of mankind to live on all the face of the earth, having determined their appointed times and the boundaries of their habitations.*

Have you ever considered that God is sovereign over where you live? As newlyweds, our daughter and son-in-law found themselves serving in a North African city, teaching English as a second language. As workers for a mission organization, they also learned the local language in hopes of sharing the gospel with the people they encountered. After two years, God called them back to the States, where they both accepted jobs with an organization in a small college town in the southern part of the country. While searching for a place to live, they "happened" to meet a family moving overseas for two years who needed to rent out their home. Shortly after moving in, they introduced themselves to their next-door neighbor and soon discovered that he was from the same city and country where they had served. He spoke the exact same dialect they had just spent two years learning. As they reached out in friendship, they realized this man was lost, practicing a false religion, and needed to hear the gospel. They were uniquely equipped to speak truth and grace into his life.

Was this coincidence? According to scripture, God had a plan, both in the places and experiences that prepared them and in directing their steps to come full circle into their neighbor's life. This is just one example of how God's sovereignty plays an important part in accomplishing His kingdom work as we obey His command to take the gospel into all the world.

Where has God put you?

Read Acts 17:24-26 again. God guides our steps in personal ways to place us where He has people who need to hear about Jesus. He determines *when* we live, and *where* we live. You might believe your own choices led you here, but a thorough examination of your life's events will reveal how God has been working in your life all along.

The first step in reaching those people is believing **that God has placed you where you are *right now*.** He has determined when and where you live for the sake of the gospel.

God has purpose in where you live, work, and play.

Luke 10:1-2 - *Now after this the Lord appointed seventy others, and sent them in pairs ahead of Him to every city and place **where He Himself was going to come**. And He was saying to them, "The harvest is plentiful, but the laborers are few; therefore beseech the Lord of the harvest to send out laborers into **His harvest**.*

Luke tells us that Jesus sent His disciples to specific cities and villages for a specific reason: He was planning a personal follow-up visit! Similarly, Jesus wants to come to your neighborhood, your office, your gym, and He has already sent you there ahead of Him, into His harvest. This harvest pertains to souls. God is actively working in hearts, and He seeks laborers to gather the harvest. He has appointed you to be the one to speak the gospel so they can respond.

Instead of asking God, "Where do you want to send me?" we must recognize that *we have already been sent.*

Don't be distracted. Don't make excuses.

Matthew 16:21-23 - *From that time Jesus began to show His disciples that He must go to Jerusalem, and suffer many things from the elders and chief priests and scribes, and be killed, and be raised up on the third day. Peter took Him aside and began to rebuke Him, saying, "God forbid it, Lord! This shall never happen to You." But He turned and said to Peter, "Get behind Me, Satan! You are a stumbling block to Me; for you are not setting your mind on God's interests, but man's."*

Peter was viewing things from the wrong perspective (his own interests) and had misplaced priorities (to save Jesus' life). Jesus understood it was his enemy, Satan's plan to divert Him from His mission (the cross). When you recognize that God has placed you where you are and begin to live on mission for Him, you will encounter distractions and be tempted to make excuses. You will need to decide whether you will live your life for God's interests or your own.

Key Truths To Remember

1. God is sovereign over where you live, work and play.
2. God has put you there for the sake of the gospel.
3. You are *already* sent into His harvest.
4. You will be distracted and want to make excuses. Don't.

Make It Practical

Where has God sent you? Where you live? Where you work? Where you play? Choose **one**. For the purposes of this guidebook, we will use "neighborhood" as our mission field; **the strategy remains the same no matter where you are**.

Create a diagram of your neighborhood in the box on the next page, including the names of the people you know. Identify those you see regularly, along with neighbors you haven't met yet. This week, make a conscious effort to personally introduce yourself to one or more of your neighbors.

Pray for God to reveal the harvest in your neighborhood and to instill His love for your neighbors in you.

Draw your diagram here:

List the names or addresses of the people you will make an intentional effort to meet this week:

_____
_____
_____
_____
_____
_____
_____
_____

STEP TWO
Pray For The People Right Around You

> **KEY SCRIPTURE: Matthew 9:35-38**
>
> *Jesus was going through all the cities and villages, teaching in their synagogues and proclaiming the gospel of the kingdom, and healing every kind of disease and every kind of sickness. Seeing the people, He felt compassion for them, because they were distressed and dispirited like sheep without a shepherd. Then He said to His disciples, "The harvest is plentiful, but the workers are few. Therefore, beseech the Lord of the harvest to send out workers into His harvest."*

Several years ago, our small group circled up around a brother in Christ who was heartbroken over his lost children. We live in North Carolina, while our friend's children live in California. As we prayed for their salvation, we also asked for someone to enter their lives to share the gospel with them and guide them to Christ. As God met us during that prayer, His Spirit spoke to my heart in His gentle, convicting manner: "There are others of My children praying for someone to share the gospel with their lost loved ones…people who are right around you. Will you be the answer to their prayers?"

This was recently brought home to me as a couple shared their struggles with our church in trying to help a wayward son and his girlfriend who had come to live with them. The son's mother reached out to the girlfriend's mother, who lived ten hours away in another state, to express her desire to lead her son and his girlfriend to Christ and to discover anything that could assist her in ministering to this young woman. The girl's mother replied that she had been praying diligently for her daughter, asking God to send someone into her life to share the message of Jesus. Our friends were the answer to that mother's prayers.

Prayer gives us God's heart for our neighbors.

Read Matthew 9:35-38 above. Jesus felt compassion for the people because He recognized their spiritual condition. They were distressed and dispirited, like sheep without a shepherd. Don't overlook the fact that Jesus noticed the people. Many times, we walk past the same individuals day after day without reflecting on their souls. We often only see what lies on the surface. As you learn to **pray** for those around *you*, you will cultivate greater compassion for them. You will share the same heart for the lost that Jesus has.

Prayer is not only something we do before we "go on mission." Prayer *is* the mission.

Acts 1:14 – *These all with one mind were continually devoting themselves to prayer, along with the women, and Mary the mother of Jesus, and with His brothers.*

After Jesus ascended into heaven, His disciples gathered in an upper room and devoted themselves to prayer for ten days. Jesus had told them they would need to be empowered by the Holy Spirit before they could fulfill His command to go and make disciples of all the nations. They did the only thing they knew to do; **they prayed**. Acts 2 tells us what happened as a result. They were filled with the Spirit and empowered to go out and tell the good news about Jesus so that all who heard it could understand it.

The story of Pentecost and the coming of the Holy Spirit is just the first of many narratives in the book of Acts, where the power of prayer precedes a great work of God. Prayer serves as a catalyst that moves God's hand. It is an invitation for God's Spirit to utilize our words, thoughts, and deeds, empowering them for significant spiritual work. Prayer is the work that must be done before we engage with our neighbors. It is a request for God to speak to our neighbors first so that they are prepared to listen when it is time for us to communicate with them.

Prayer puts us where the Lord wants us.

In Acts 8, Philip was walking with a heart eager to share the gospel with anyone God placed in his path. God directed him to the desert road in Gaza, where He had a divine appointment arranged with an Ethiopian eunuch. Philip heeded the guidance of the Holy Spirit and was able to clearly explain the gospel to this man, whose heart was already prepared by God. The result was salvation.

Philip is a great example of **prayer walking,** an opportunity to invite God into the lives of our neighbors. By walking through your neighborhood, praying as you go, and stopping to chat when you meet a neighbor, you create opportunities to gain *insight* while *on site*. Not only will you meet neighbors who don't know Christ, but you will also meet other believers whom you can invite to begin praying with you for your neighborhood.

Prayer walking...
- Focuses your thoughts so that you can be intentional in your prayers.
- Disciplines your mind to listen to God's Spirit as you walk.
- Gives you opportunities to meet your neighbors.
- Provides a structured, sustained method of praying for neighbors.

When we pray, we are asking God to open the hearts of our neighbors and give them spiritual eyes to see and hear truth.

Acts 16:14 – *A woman named Lydia, from the city of Thyatira, a seller of purple fabrics, a worshiper of God, was listening; and the Lord opened her heart to respond to the things spoken by Paul.*

As Paul and his companions went "prayer walking" from city to city, they encountered individuals where God was already at work. We refer to these as "people of peace." (See Luke 10:6) Lydia exemplified a person of peace; her heart was receptive to the things of God, but she needed someone to share the message of Jesus with her. God orchestrated her meeting with Paul in a divine manner. She responded and received salvation. This is what we pray for!

Key Truths To Remember

1. Prayer isn't something you only do *before* the mission; prayer is your mission.
2. Praying to the Lord of the harvest gives you *His heart* for the lost.
3. Listening is as important as asking; learn to be Spirit-led.
4. Prayer walking gives insight while you are "on-site."
5. God has already prepared people of peace for you to meet, and someone is praying for them. Be the answer to their prayers.

Make It Practical

Pray daily for the **p**eople **a**round **y**ou by name. Go on a prayer walk. As you encounter other believers, enlist them to join you. Organize your neighborhood among fellow believers so that everyone is being prayed for by name each day. Write the names of the people you are praying for below.

_____

_____

_____

_____

_____

_____

STEP THREE
Look For Needs And Act On Them When The Spirit Leads

> **KEY SCRIPTURE: Matthew 5:16**
>
> *Let your light shine before men in such a way that they may see your good works, and glorify your Father who is in heaven.*

We love hearing stories of how God speaks clearly to His children. Several years ago, we held a workshop with a group of about twenty-five believers, including one of the associate pastors from the hosting church. We met weekly for six weeks. About halfway through, after covering the sessions on praying by name for our neighbors, the associate pastor shared that God had a sense of humor in answering his prayer. He had started praying specifically for his next-door neighbors, a couple who had always been unfriendly. He had tried to reach out before, with little success. After he began praying diligently and intentionally, a storm swept through their neighborhood and caused his neighbor's tree to fall on his fence.

Because he had been praying, he recognized this as a God-given opportunity to respond with grace. Instead of confronting the neighbor with the same unfriendly attitude he expected, he offered kindness and even helped remove the tree. He noted that the neighbor's attitude had dramatically changed and was now open to a growing friendship. He was praying that God would soon open the door to share the gospel with his new friend.

God often works in unexpected ways. When we faithfully pray for those right around us, we need to be aware of and watch for the opportunities He will surely orchestrate to answer our prayers.

We meet needs for God's glory, not ours.

Read Matthew 5:16 above. Just before this verse, Jesus tells His disciples that they are to be **salt** and **light** as citizens of the kingdom of heaven. When seen and experienced by our neighbors, our good deeds should not reflect how good we are but cause them to thirst for Christ and reveal who He is. Our actions should bring glory to God.

As we pray for others and listen to the Holy Spirit's leading, we will notice their physical needs. As we meet those needs, we will have the opportunity to tell our neighbors about the One who can meet their spiritual needs.

Who is your neighbor?

Luke 10:36-37 — *"Which of these three do you think proved to be a neighbor to the man who fell into the robbers' hands?" And he said, "The one who showed mercy toward him." Then Jesus said to him, "Go and do the same."*

In Luke 10:25-37, Jesus addresses a crucial question for us. A lawyer, seeking to justify his own righteousness, asks, "Who is my neighbor?" This question arises in response to Jesus' command that we should love God first and foremost, and love our neighbor as ourselves. Jesus then recounts the well-known story of the Good Samaritan.

A man on a journey is attacked by robbers, beaten, and left for dead. Three people pass by: a priest, a Levite, and a Samaritan. The priest and the Levite, both religious figures, ignore the man's needs and continue walking. The Samaritan, however, *loves the man as he loves himself.* He does what he would want someone to do for him. He feels compassion and shows mercy, meeting the physical needs of the injured man by taking time from his schedule, ministering to him with his own hands, and using his personal resources. The Samaritan was the only one who understood what Jesus was saying: **"Your neighbor is whoever is in front of you,"** and "You love your neighbor as yourself as you meet his needs."

Meeting needs involves compassion, care and commitment.

There was one difference between the Samaritan and the other two men: he recognized a divine opportunity when it presented itself. He didn't allow his personal prejudices, fear of rejection, or the obligations of his schedule to keep him from meeting the needs of someone in pain. He embraced the role that God had given him and adjusted his plans for the day to help.

If we sincerely pray for those around us, God will provide us with open doors and opportunities to engage in their lives.

Our role is to be aware of when it happens and to act. We must be willing to step outside our comfort zones and show compassion, care, and commitment, especially when it means sacrificing our own agendas.

Who is in front of you today?
Do you recognize their needs?

Key Truths To Remember

1. Your neighbor is "anyone who is in front of you."
2. Meeting physical needs will open doors for spiritual conversations.
3. God orchestrates sovereign, divine appointments.
4. Your good works are only good for eternal purposes when they bring glory to God.

Make It Practical

Ask yourself, *who has God placed on my heart to reach out to this week?* Write down three practical ways to engage this person through either a good deed or acts of mercy. Act on one of these ideas.

A few ideas to get you started...

- Invite your neighbor for a meal or take a meal to a sick neighbor.
- Visit with an elderly neighbor; offer to drive him (or her) to the store or pick up something they need.

- Offer to help while your neighbors are out of town: mow their grass, pick up their mail, take out their trash on trash pick-up day.
- Send a card to a widow or widower, letting them know you are thinking of them.
- Offer to babysit for a young couple's date night.

Are you praying for your neighbors and co-workers every day? Have you reached out to other believers and invited them to join you? Have you gone on a prayer walk?

STEP FOUR
Tell Them About Jesus

KEY SCRIPTURE: Luke 19:1-10

He entered Jericho and was passing through. And there was a man called by the name of Zaccheus; he was a chief tax collector and he was rich. Zaccheus was trying to see who Jesus was, and was unable because of the crowd, for he was small in stature. So he ran on ahead and climbed up into a sycamore tree in order to see Him, for He was about to pass through that way. When Jesus came to the place, He looked up and said to him, "Zaccheus, hurry and come down, for today I must stay at your house." And he hurried and came down and received Him gladly. When they saw it, they all began to grumble, saying, "He has gone to be the guest of a man who is a sinner." Zaccheus stopped and said to the Lord, "Behold, Lord, half of my possessions I will give to the poor, and if I have defrauded anyone of anything, I will give back four times as much." And Jesus said to him, "Today salvation has come to this house, because he, too, is a son of Abraham. For the Son of Man has come to seek and to save that which was lost."

While visiting Boston, we met a young man walking across the campus of Northeastern University. He approached us and asked if we needed any help. I suppose that three older people in their fifties didn't blend in very well, especially since it seemed to be orientation day for new students and the campus was filled with fresh-faced 18-year-olds ready to take on the world.

If I were to describe him, I would have to use the word "Shaggy" in a Scooby-Doo kind of way. His smile was genuine, and his eyes sparkled. He mentioned that he was heading home to spend time with his grandfather. Like many college students, he was very willing to discuss what young men and women his age want out of life. Words like "community" and "unity" soon opened the door for Todd to share his own story of salvation, highlighting the true unity that comes through Christ, and how he could attain that through the gospel. As Todd spoke, we prayed silently for God to open his eyes and his heart to what he was hearing.

He listened intently, answered Todd's questions, and said it was good that Todd believed that and that he "appreciated him being willing to share it." We walked away praying that God would take the seeds of the gospel that were dropped into a heart surrounded by a hostile culture, knowing that God's word never returns void.

We must speak the gospel.

Up to this point, the steps we've discussed have been relatively easy to implement. As followers of Christ, it is natural for us to be kind to others and to meet needs as they arise. We may need to stretch ourselves to reach out to our neighbors, but once we begin praying for them, our hearts change, and we start to love them as Jesus loves.

Now, we come to the most difficult challenge: How do we introduce them to Jesus? Statistics tell us that most believers agree that we should talk about the gospel, but few of us do. Let's change that statistic.

Here are three simple steps to keep in mind when you have a chance to discuss your faith with someone:

Listen, Tell, Share

1. *Listen* to their stories by asking good questions.
2. *Tell* your own story and how Jesus has changed your life.
3. *Share* the complete gospel so they understand how they can know Jesus, too.

Good questions can shift a conversation to spiritual topics.

John 4:7-10 – *There came a woman of Samaria to draw water. Jesus said to her, "Give Me a drink." For His disciples had gone away into the city to buy food. Therefore the Samaritan woman said to Him, "How is it that You, being a Jew, ask me for a drink since I am a Samaritan woman?" (For Jews have no dealings with Samaritans.) Jesus answered and said to her, "If you knew the gift of God, and who it is who says to you, 'Give Me a drink,' you would have asked Him, and He would have given you living water."*

Jesus was the master at guiding conversations toward the kingdom of God. In His encounter with the woman at the well, we can observe a straightforward strategy for steering discussions toward the gospel.

Surface questions lead to
  Personal questions, which lead to
    Religious questions, which lead to
      Spiritual questions, which lead to
        The **Gospel!**

The whole conversation can be read in the rest of John 4. Jesus began with a **surface** question: He asked for a drink of water. The conversation about water led to a **personal** question about her husband. Jesus' interest in her personal life led to a **religious** discussion: Jews and Samaritans worship differently. The religious discussion allowed Jesus to move to the **spiritual** issue in question: He revealed Himself as Messiah.

After you've listened to the other person's story, ask for permission to share yours.

Read Zaccheus' story in our Key Scripture, Luke 19. His story helps us identify four components we need to cover when sharing our own story of salvation. We see his life before meeting Jesus: he was a wealthy chief tax collector who took from his own people. We see that God was drawing him. In fact, his desire to meet Jesus was so strong he was willing to embarrass himself by running ahead and climbing a tree. We witness the true miracle: **Jesus saw Zaccheus** and invited him to come down. This was Zaccheus' moment of salvation; he responded to Jesus' invitation and obeyed. We observe how his life changed after meeting Jesus: he immediately knew he should give back what he had stolen and offer restitution beyond that.

You can share your story in 5 to 7 minutes by using these same four components:

What was my life like before I met Jesus?
How did I know I needed Jesus?
What happened when I met Jesus?
How has my life changed since I met Jesus?

Invite others to Jesus by sharing the simple, complete gospel. Make it personal for them.

After sharing your story, ask the person you're speaking with if they've ever experienced something similar. You might discover they're a Christ-follower too! If not, you can smoothly transition into a straightforward presentation of the gospel.

The gospel doesn't begin at the cross. The cross only makes sense to a person once they comprehend the need for it. When we share the story of Jesus, we must start at the beginning. These four words will help us:

Creation ⇨ Fall ⇨ Redemption ⇨ Restoration.

Creation – We were created perfectly, designed by God for an intimate, holy relationship with Him.

Fall – Adam and Eve sinned, which separated us from God and brought spiritual and physical death into our world.

Redemption – Jesus, God's Son, entered our world as a human baby, lived a perfect, sinless life, died on the cross to pay our sin debt, and was raised from the grave, conquering death and offering eternal life to those who believe.

Restoration – Jesus' death and resurrection reconcile us back to God, returning us to our original design. We are spiritually restored now, and one day we will enjoy eternity with physically restored bodies, living in the presence of God forever.

If someone is open to listening, you can read Bible verses together that explain and affirm what you've shared. If they are ready to accept Christ, they will let you know. If not, pray with them for God to grant them understanding. If feasible, arrange to meet with them again.

Jesus is the only way of salvation.

Acts 4:12 – *And there is salvation in no one else; for there is no other name under heaven that has been given among men by which we must be saved.*

If you do not believe that people will perish without a saving faith in Jesus, you will not feel compelled to share the gospel. However, if you believe what the Bible teaches, you must respond to Jesus' command to *"Go and make disciples."* (Matthew 28:19)

You can be equipped to share the gospel with people right around you—those who live, work, and play in your neighborhood and community—individuals whom God has already positioned in your life. We pray that this is the desire of your heart and that many believers will enter the kingdom because of your faithful commitment to sharing the gospel.

> **Key Truths To Remember**
>
> 1. If we know Jesus, we are commanded to share the gospel.
> 2. Jesus is the only way to salvation; people will perish apart from Christ.
> 3. You have a story to tell. Be ready to tell it.
> 4. Share the complete gospel: creation, fall, redemption, restoration.
> 5. Strive to have intentional, purposeful conversations.
> 6. Learn to listen.

Make It Practical

Write your story of salvation in the space below, including the four points of the complete gospel in your own words. Practice sharing it with others until you feel comfortable and confident. Ask God to reveal to you who you are meant to share the gospel with, both in words and actions. Pray for that person, and then act when God orchestrates the right time and place.

_____
_____
_____
_____
_____
_____
_____
_____
_____
_____
_____
_____

Now What?

We hope that this little guidebook inspires you to share the gospel and equips you to feel confident and called to do so. We are asking God to raise up Christ-followers who will accept the challenge to be that **O**NE who knows they are **O**bligated to their **N**eighbor's **E**ternity.

So, now what? You can start implementing the steps in this book today without any additional training. However, if you want to delve deeper into the biblical principles we've presented, **we offer a five-session Bible study workbook** that is ideal for small groups. This is a great "next step" as you connect with other believers in your neighborhood and take the initiative to reach the mission field where God has placed you. (You can find the *Going Around The Corner* **Bible** study on our website; details are in the Appendix.)

The Appendix also provides expanded information. *Around The Corner Ministries* offers workshops for local churches and other resources that support our mission to **take the gospel to every neighborhood in America.**

We hope to hear from you!

Around The Corner Ministries
Todd & Sheila Alewine
aroundthecornerministries.org
todd@aroundthecornerministries.org

APPENDIX

TURNING CONVERSATIONS TOWARD CHRIST

Here's a straightforward formula for engaging others in conversations that lead to the gospel.

First, **explore** by opening doors to learn as much as possible about the person. We accomplish this using two types of questions that build upon one another.

Surface Questions:
Where did you grow up?
What brought you to this location?
What sports do you like?
What are your hobbies?

Personal Questions:
Are you married?
Do you have children?
Do you have pets?
Where do you work?
Where are places you have traveled?

Second, **engage** by steering your conversation toward the gospel. Use the third type of question to discover spiritual interest and to serve as a bridge to deeper inquiries. Consider this a "pivot" question.

Religious Questions:
What did you do on the weekends growing up?
Did you attend church as a child?
Did you get married at a church?
Do you ever think about spiritual things?
What are your beliefs about faith?

Finally, **evangelize.** If the person is open and genuinely seeking the Lord—a *person of peace*—then move on to the fourth type of question.

Spiritual Questions:
What do you think about Jesus?
Are you a Christian?
What does "Christian" mean to you?
Do you have a personal relationship with Jesus?
Can I tell you my story of how I met Jesus?
Can I share with you how you can begin a relationship with Jesus?

If someone is willing to hear your story, be sure to integrate the complete gospel as you share. If time and setting allow, read the scriptures together and let God's work speak. Your role is not to convince but to proclaim the message and invite. God's Spirit will do His part.

How To Become A Christ-Follower

Believe that God created you for a relationship with Him.
Genesis 1:27 – *God created man in His own image, in the image of God He created him; male and female He created them.*
Colossians 1:16 – *For by Him all things were created, both in the heavens and on earth, visible and invisible, whether thrones or dominions or rulers or authorities - all things have been created through Him and for Him.*

Admit that you are separated from God because of your sin.
Romans 3:23 - *For all have sinned and fall short of the glory of God.*

Repent by confessing and turning away from your sin.
1 John 1:9 – *If we confess our sins, He is faithful and righteous to forgive us our sins and to cleanse us from all unrighteousness.*

Accept that Jesus died for your sin debt and rose from the grave.
Romans 5:8-9 – *But God demonstrates His own love toward us, in that while we were yet sinners, Christ died for us. Much more then, having now been justified by His blood, we shall be saved from the wrath of God through Him.*
Romans 10:9-10 – *That if you confess with your mouth Jesus as Lord, and believe in your heart that God raised Him from the dead, you will be saved; for with the heart a person believes, resulting in righteousness, and with the mouth he confesses, resulting in salvation.*

Receive Jesus in to control your life through the Holy Spirit.
John 1:12 – *But as many as received Him, to them He gave the right to become children of God, even to those who believe in His name.*

What To Pray
Dear Jesus, I recognize that I am separated from You because of my personal sin, and I need Your forgiveness. I believe that You died on the cross to pay the penalty for my sin. I confess my sin and ask You to forgive me. By faith, I repent and turn from my way of life to follow You

instead. I accept Your gift of salvation by grace. I ask You to come into my life and transform me. Thank You for saving me and giving me eternal life. Amen.

If you sincerely prayed this prayer and surrendered your life to God, you are now His child. Please share this decision with another believer and ask them to guide you in living your new life in Christ. We would love to hear from you regarding your decision.

Additional Resources

aroundthecornerministries.org

Be Strategic With The Gospel

Going Around The Corner Bible Study
ISBN: 9780692781999 / List Price: $12.99
This five-session workbook helps believers explore the mission field in their own neighborhoods and workplaces. Learn to engage others through prayer and biblical good works guided by the prompts of the Holy Spirit. Gain confidence to evangelize through sharing the complete gospel and your own story. Discover how to establish and equip new believers in their faith journey. A simple, practical, and biblical strategy for disciple-making.

Going Around The Corner Bible Study, Leader Guide
ISBN: 9780999131824 / List Price: $3.99
Key truths for each week, helpful discussion starters, and thoughtful questions to assist your group in applying the principles from the study, along with suggested group activities and practical application steps. Adaptable for use with the Student Edition.

Be Aware Of The Gospel

40 Days of Spiritual Awareness
ISBN: 9780999131800 / List Price: $9.99
A devotional to help you understand who God is and how He is working in the people around you. Discover truths that will increase your awareness of God, yourself, other believers, and unbelievers. Be reminded of what matters: being aware of God's work in our world as He redeems and saves. By the end of the journey, you will realize that you play an important role in accomplishing that work and will be ready to join Him.

Be Refreshed In The Gospel

Grace & Glory: A 50-Day Journey In The Purpose & Plan Of God
ISBN: 9780999131848 / List Price $11.99
What should we do when we face a crisis of faith? When everything we believe is challenged? That's when we need to discover (or rediscover) God's purpose for our lives and learn to live with a mindset of His grace... grace that reveals His glory. This devotional will refresh believers in the gospel and encourage them to live each day so that the glory of God will be proclaimed through the power of grace at work in their lives.

More resources can be found on our website!